Dug

the Groundhog

PAGE PUBLISHING
Conneaut Lake, PA

First originally published by Page Publishing 2023

ISBN 979-8-88654-096-3 (pbk)
ISBN 979-8-88654-105-2 (digital)

Printed in the United States of America

Dug

the Groundhog

James R. Hale

Mr. Hale lives in the suburb of Indianapolis and loves to grow food in his garden. He has a really small yard, so he makes good use of raised beds and what he calls vertical gardening. Even though he only has a little space to grow things, he does manage to grow a lot of vegetables. He grows things like tomatoes, green beans, potatoes, beets, cucumbers, onions, broccoli, jalapeños, bell peppers, and a variety of spices.

3

Mr. Hale works hard to maintain his garden. It takes many hours of work before he can even start to plant any seeds. He has to get the soil ready by adding the right fertilizers and turning the soil over and over to get it ground up so it is nice and fluffy. After he gets the soil ready, then he can start mounding up his soil into rows. Mr. Hale is really picky about how straight his rows are. He does a lot of math to help him figure out how many rows he can fit into his little area. Also, if he knows how many rows he can put in, then he will know how many plants he can put in his garden.

Mr. Hale then gets the right number of seeds to plant in his nice and straight rows. He is real careful and makes sure to put those seeds in at the right depth and spaced far enough apart. They have to have room to grow. After putting in the seeds, he must give them plenty of water. Everything that grows needs water. After a while, the seeds will start growing, and Mr. Hale will start seeing green leaves poking through the soil. In the summer, it gets very hot, so the garden will need watering every day. He will also spend a lot of time pulling unwanted plants that grow called weeds. Those weeds are really hard to keep under control because Mr. Hale doesn't like to use weed-killing chemicals. Not only does the garden attract weeds but also it attracts bugs and animals like rabbits, gofers, and groundhogs. Wow! Having a garden takes a lot of time and can be hard work at times. However, growing a garden brings much joy to Mr. Hale and is good exercise for him. Until one day, he met Dug the Groundhog.

Dug the Groundhog lives with his mom and dad and two sisters under Mr. Hale's shed that is in the backyard. Dug has many relatives who live in the same neighborhood, and they have dug many tunnels throughout the community. Dug is a very social groundhog, so he is always traveling around the neighborhood, visiting his family and friends, and looking for food. Sometimes he likes to go across Shortridge Road to see some other friends that he goes to school with. On the other side of the street, they have many berries and fruit trees that they like to eat from. One time, they were enjoying the food so much that they lost track of where they were and ended up way out by Highway 40. The street is very busy. They got scared and ran all the way back home.

Meanwhile, the plants in Mr. Hale's garden are starting to grow and are looking really good. There are many colors in the garden now that the vegetables are starting to bloom, and Dug the Groundhog becomes curious. Dug decided to investigate the garden a little closer and walked over to the first row. The first row of plants he came to were tomatoes. As he was looking at the tomatoes, he noticed how bright red they were. He moved a little closer to get a sniff of one tomato. Dug was thinking, *Boy, they look good and smell good! I wonder how they taste!*

He grabbed one with his mouth and started eating it. "Wow!" he said. "That tastes great." And he ate it all the way down to the core.

The next day, Dug ventured back into Mr. Hale's garden to find some more delicious food. In a different row of plants, he came across something new. He found some broccoli. Without even thinking about it too much, he just snatched one of the leaves off the plant and started eating it. They were so good. He ate several pieces. In another row, he was pleased to find something different. He quickly figured out that every row had something amazingly different. This made Dug very happy.

For the next several weeks, Dug and his friends and family ate real good out of Mr. Hale's garden. They had almost eaten everything out of the garden. It was a mess.

    As Dug and his friends enjoyed eating out of
Mr. Hale's garden, Mr. Hale started to notice that
something was eating the food out of his garden.
This made Mr. Hale very angry, and he started to
keep a closer eye on his garden. He had worked
really hard making his garden, and he was not
going to let anything destroy it any more than it
already had.

One morning, while watering the plants, Mr. Hale saw Dug crawling under his shed.

"Uh-huh!" he said. "I see you! You little groundhog. You are probably what is eating up all my vegetables," he mumbled, "I will put an end to this."

He walked to the shed and opened the door. He reached in and pulled out a cage. It was a hunter's trap. Dug, hiding under the shed, saw Mr. Hale open the door and pull something out. He had no idea what that was. Mr. Hale took that trap over by his tomato plant and sat it down and grabbed a tomato off of the plant and threw it in the cage. He messed with the cage for a few minutes and then walked away.

Dug, still watching from under the shed, saw the tomato that Mr. Hale put in the cage and started feeling a bit hungry. He looked to make sure Mr. Hale was gone and moved slowly over to where the tomato was lying in the cage.

"Nice!" Dug said, "Mr. Hale picked me a tomato to eat!"

In order for him to get the tomato, he had to find his way into the cage. Dug tried to get the tomato several different ways. Finally, he found his way to the tomato. As he moved quickly into the cage to get the tomato, he heard a noise and the ground under his feet rumbled. He got scared for a second, but his mouth was watering for the taste of that tomato. It is his favorite thing to eat from the garden. In a few minutes, Dug had eaten that tomato and turned to leave, but the way out of the cage was blocked.

Dug was trapped in the cage, and no matter how hard he tried, he could not get out. After a while, the sun started to go down and Dug desperately wanted to get out. He tried and tried and tried until he was so tired he could even hardly stand up. So he just fell asleep.

The next day when he woke up, he was still trapped.
Suddenly, he heard a voice. It was Mr. Hale's voice saying,
"I got you, little groundhog, and now you are going for a
ride in my truck."

Mr. Hale picked up the cage with Dug in it and carried it over to the bed of the truck. Several hours went by before Mr. Hale backed his truck out of the driveway and drove away from his house. By this time, Dug was getting really hungry, but there was no food for him to eat. All he could do was sit in the back of the truck and watch the stars come out.

As he sat watching those stars, he noticed that one was really bright and another one that was almost as bright, and some were all bunched together in one spot.

Out of all the stars he saw, he noticed that the bright one seemed to always be following him. Whichever way Mr. Hale turned his truck, that star was right over him.

As Dug stayed busy looking at stars, Mr. Hale drove Dug to the woods that were on the opposite side of the city. When the truck stopped, Dug had no idea where he was. Mr. Hale picked up the cage and walked over to the grass on the edge of the woods. Suddenly, the door opened, and Dug ran out into the woods. Scared to death, Dug sat in one spot under a bush and watched Mr. Hale drive away. The only thing Dug could think of was home.

"How can I get back home to see my mom, dad, and sisters?" he asked.

Then he remembered the star that followed him when he was in the back of Mr. Hale's truck. He looked up into the night sky, and there it was. Still following him.

He asked the star, "Star, do you know the way to my house? You followed me all the way here, you must know the way back."

Of course, the star did not talk back, but it did turn off and on real quick as if it was trying to say, "Yes, I do know the way home."

Dug heard a noise in the woods and turned to see what it was. He did not see anything behind him. He was scared and did not know what to do, so he just started running in the direction that he saw Mr. Hale drive away. He ran and ran and ran until he needed to catch his breath. He found some tall grass to lay down in.

As he lay there resting, he noticed that the star was still there, but it was a little way in front of him. He started to walk to the star. As Dug got closer to the star, the star moved away from him. The star was guiding Dug home.

Dug followed that star through the night, and soon the star's brightness began to fade.

"Oh no!" Dug shouted. "What will I do without my guiding light?"

Soon the sun came up, and the star was gone. When the sun came up, Dug realized he could see a lot better. He took a glance around to see where he was and realized he was not far from Highway 40. He remembered this street when he and his friends got lost in a field eating berries one day. Dug has to figure out how to get to the other side of that street.

It's a really busy street, and he could get hit by a car if he is not careful.

"I am a fast runner," said Dug, "I think I will run for it. It would take several days for me to dig a tunnel under the street."

So Dug watched and watched for the right moment to run for it. Finally, he had a chance and ran as fast as he could. Halfway across, he saw a car heading right for him.

"Oh no!" he yelled. He ran a few more steps and dove, just barely avoiding the car's front tire. He rolled off to the side of the road. Looking up, he found out he had made it to the other side of the road.

"Yahoo! Yahoo!" he yelled. "I found my way home! Thank you, my guiding light!"

Dug ran to the end of the field. His friend that he goes to see who lives on the other side of Shortridge saw him.

"Hey, Dug! Can you play?" he asked.

"Not now, I have to get home. I was trapped and taken far away last night, and I am just now finding my way home. My mom and dad must be worried about me."

"Yes," his friend said, "your parents were over here looking for you yesterday."

"They were?" Dug asked. "I will see you later," Dug said as he turned and jumped into the tunnel that led to his community.

It didn't take Dug long to get to his house. When he got to the end of his tunnel, he slowly poked his head out to see if Mr. Hale was around. Mr. Hale was nowhere in sight. Still hungry from the night before, Dug grabbed a nice big red tomato as he ran past Mr. Hale's garden. When he got home, his parents were so happy to see him. They hugged him and gave him kisses and asked him where he had been. He told them the whole story and how that bright star guided him home. He told them how thankful he was to be home.

Later that night, Dug was sitting comfortably under Mr. Hale's shed. Poking his head out from under the shed just enough to see that bright star that guided him home, he smiled and thanked it once again.

About the Author

James Hale was born on January 28, 1970, in downtown Indianapolis, Indiana. He went to the school for adult learning at the University of Indianapolis, where he received his bachelor's degree in liberal studies in 2014 at the age of forty-six. James is married and has three adult children. James enjoys fishing, traveling, and cooking on his grill.

www.ingramcontent.com/pod-product-compliance
Lightning Source LLC
Chambersburg PA
CBHW041822110726
48006CB00019B/2473